SPONSORSHIP PAGE

THIS BOOK IS SPONSORED BY

....

....

AS A GIFT TO

....

....

ON THIS DAY

....

'Each one must give as he has decided in his heart,
not reluctantly or under compulsion,
for God loves a cheerful giver.'
(2 Corinthians 9:7, ESV)

CONTAINS POWERFUL DECREES TO DESTROY
COLLECTIVE CAPTIVITY & UNREPENTANT KILLERS

The FALSE PROPHET

EXPOSING THE AGENDA, SECRETS & ACTS
OF THE FALSE PROPHETS

PRAYER M. MADUEKE

PRAYER
PUBLICATIONS
UNITED STATES

© 2022 Prayer M. Madueke

ISBN: 979-8838721501

1st Edition

All Scripture quotations are taken from the King James Version of the Bible, and used by permission. All emphasis within quotations is the author's additions.

Published by Prayer Publications.

This book and all other Prayer Publications books are available at Christian bookstores and distributors worldwide.

This book and all other Prayer Publications books may be purchased in bulk for educational, business, fundraising, or sales promotional use. For information, please email hello@theprayerpublications.com.

Reach us on the internet: www.theprayerpublications.com.

For Worldwide Distribution,
Printed in the United States of America.

FREE EBOOKS

In order to say a 'Thank You' for purchasing *The False Prophet*, I offer these books to you in appreciation.

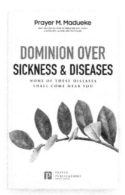
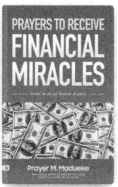

> **> Click here or go to madueke.com/free-gift to download the eBooks now <**

MESSAGE FROM THE AUTHOR

PRAYER M. MADUEKE
CHRISTIAN AUTHOR

My name is Prayer Madueke, a spiritual warrior in the Lord's vineyard, an accomplished author, speaker, and expert on spiritual warfare and deliverance. I have published well over 100 books on every area of successful Christian living. I am an acclaimed family and relationship counselor with several titles dealing with critical areas in the lives of the children of God. I travel to several countries each year speaking and conducting deliverance sessions, breaking the yokes of demonic oppression and setting captives free.

It would be a delight to collaborate with you or your ministry in organized crusades, ceremonies, marriages and marriage seminars, special events, church ministration and fellowship for the advancement of God's kingdom here on earth.

You can find all my books on my website: madueke.com.

They have produced many testimonies and I want your testimony to be one too. God bless you.

CHRISTIAN COUNSELLING

We were created for a greater purpose than only survival and God wants us to live a full life.

If you need prayer or counselling, or if you have any other inquiries, please visit the counselling page on my website madueke.com/counselling to know when I will be available for a phone call.

TABLE OF CONTENTS

Chapter One

Warning from The True Prophet 1

Chapter Two

Progress in your Community 14

— Your Role in your Community 19

Chapter Three

Discerning False Prophets 21

— The Woman in Charge of Falsehood 23

Chapter Four

Victory Over Satanic Prophets 29

— Training School for True Liberation 31

— Bible Passages To Read 32

Warfare Section

— Decrees for Deliverance from Personal Idol 35

— Decrees against Family Idols 37

— Decrees against Community Idols 39

— Decrees against Collective Captivity 41

— Decrees against Tribal Idols 43

— Decrees against all Problems 44

— Decrees to Overthrow Mediocrity 46

- Decrees to Prosper In Any Community........................... 48
- Decrees against Occultism 50
- Decrees against Unrepentant Killers 51
- Decrees against Strongman... 53
- Decrees for Divine Presence 55
- Decrees for your Deliverance 56
- Decrees for Peace in the Land.. 57
- Decrees of Judgment in the Land... 60

ONE

WARNING FROM THE TRUE PROPHET

J esus Christ, the true prophet of God who can see hidden
things even in the dark, sent letters to the seven churches in
Asia. In the letters, He commended, warned, rebuked,
encouraged and extended His promises to all who had ears to
hear.

Here, we are studying His message (letter) to the community
church in Thyatira. In this church, Christ saw a false prophetess
who had been teaching and wrongly influencing the members.

> And unto the angel of the church in Thyatira write;
> These things saith the Son of God, who hath his eyes
> like unto a flame of fire, and his feet are like fine brass;
>
> — REVELATION 2:18

For a very long time, this false prophetess with the spirit of Jezebel had deceived many in the community undetected. She occupied a prominent position in the church and was accorded recognition by the community leadership. Her teachings influenced many into adopting her sinful lifestyle. All the teachers and leaders in Thyatira were under her influence. They were possessed by the spirit of Jezebel.

> And he shall send Jesus Christ, which before was preached unto you:
>
> Whom the heaven must receive until the times of restitution of all things, which God hath spoken by the mouth of all his holy prophets since the world began.
>
> For Moses truly said unto the fathers, A prophet shall the Lord your God raise up unto you of your brethren, like unto me; him shall ye hear in all things whatsoever he shall say unto you.

> And it shall come to pass, that every soul, which will not hear that prophet, shall be destroyed from among the people.
>
> — ACTS 3:20-23

Christ, His eyes like a flaming with fire, saw this false prophetess in the fullness of her deceit and destructive ministry. With a letter, He walked into the church with feet of brass. As the true and faithful prophet of God, He confronted this false prophetess, something no one had done before.

If you are wreaking havoc in your community unchallenged, Christ is here with a warning letter for you.

If you have influenced people in your church with your sinful lifestyle and wicked acts, yet no one has dared to preach to you, open your ears. If you promote sin, wickedness everywhere, yet none has rebuked you, Christ, the true prophet of God, is not afraid of you.

If you have authority in your community church but influence people to do evil, you have a warning letter from Christ. If you practice witchcraft, poison people, bewitch and waste destinies but never been rebuked, Christ is sending you a warning letter

3

today. If you're misusing your authority or position, a warning letter from Christ awaits you.

You may have access to church money through your witchcraft, this may be your last or only warning letter. The truth is that this rebuke or warning letter is coming from the faithful Prophet of God. If you have despised other rebukes and warnings and got away with them, this one is coming from heaven, the faithful Prophet of God. This preaching is coming from Christ, the one whom all prophets spoke about since the world began. The Prophet that Moses saw and told the fathers of Israel that God will raise as a Prophet. The Prophet that Moses commanded us to listen to in all things.

No matter your position in the occult, you must listen to Him. You may be a leader in your family, place of work or community, you must listen to Him. You may be the general overseer; you must listen to Him. You may be an archbishop, an apostle, the leader of other leaders, you must hear Him. You may run your community's resources as a personal business, you must hear Him now. You may have lived this way all your life, influencing people wrongly, this time, you must hear Him.

You may have mismanaged the ministry, and people under you, lived like Jezebel, you must listen to Christ now. Whether you read this letter or not, every disobedient person will be judged.

For those who are privileged to read this letter, obedience is demanded from you. You may have despised other letters and gone free; you must not despise this one. The author is Christ, the one that Moses instructed the fathers of Israel to obey. No matter how old you are, or your place in the occult, you are not older than the fathers of Israel.

This is a Prophet recognized by God, from heaven, approved by the Almighty, spoken about by Moses, respected by the fathers of Israel. He is the true and faithful Prophet, raised by God.

> For mine eyes are upon all their ways: they are not hid from my face, neither is their iniquity hid from mine eyes.
>
> Can any hide himself in secret places that I shall not see him? saith the Lord. Do not I fill heaven and earth? saith the Lord.
>
> — JEREMIAH 16:17; 23:24

You may have all the nine gifts of the Holy Spirit (healing, miracle, prophecy etc.), you must hear this Prophet. You may be intelligent, highly respected and revered, you must hear this Prophet. You may have attacked your enemies in the community with stroke, wasted their children and aborted great destinies, you will not succeed this time.

You may have dominated everyone in your community, and caused unborn children of your enemies to become imbeciles, you cannot continue. If you do not listen to and obey this Prophet, you will be destroyed from among the people. Whatever you have achieved in life, and no matter your contributions, you must pay attention to this Prophet.

Moses instructed the fathers of Israel to listen to whatsoever He shall say. Christ is that Prophet, the faithful and steadfast Prophet from God, raised by God and commissioned to write to me and you and we must hear. No matter where you have gone in the past or where you will go in the future, His eyes are seeing you clearly.

None of your wickedness is hidden from His eyes. He sees all. There is no iniquity that can be hidden from His eyes. All your past is exposed before Him. Every activity going on in your occult altars, or witchcraft covens is exposed to His eyes. You have no option than to come before Him in repentance and ask for forgiveness.

He revealeth the deep and secret things: he knoweth
what is in the darkness, and the light dwelleth with
him.

— DANIEL 2:22

And it shall come to pass at that time, that I will search
Jerusalem with candles, and punish the men that are
settled on their lees: that say in their heart, The Lord
will not do good, neither will he do evil.

— ZEPHANIAH 1:12

It is foolishness to think or believe that you have a secret before
God. He knows your evil activities, the people you have killed
or whom you have destroyed their business in your community.
This letter is telling you to acknowledge your sins and repent.

Your darkest or deepest secrets are exposed before the eyes of
this faithful Prophet. He is light and light lives with Him and
can never be separated from Him. The eyes of Christ are the
source of all-seeing eyes and the candles of the world put
together.

And needed not that any should testify of man: for he
knew what was in man.

— JOHN 2:25

Neither is there any creature that is not manifest in his
sight: but all things are naked and opened unto the
eyes of him with whom we have to do.

— HEBREWS 4:13

This Prophet has no need to search, ask questions, investigate,
or enquire of anyone's activity before He knows it. He knows
all men, their past, their present and their end from the
beginning.

His head and his hairs were white like wool, as white
as snow; and his eyes were as a flame of fire;

And his feet like unto fine brass, as if they burned in a
furnace; and his voice as the sound of many waters.

— REVELATION 1:14-15

Christ has eyes like the flames of a fire and can see all things without obstruction. What He is saying is that He is still in charge of every community, not you or your witchcraft group. He will judge everyone who refuses to obey. If you are gifted to heal, deliver or prophesy, Christ is saying, you need to know that all gifts come from Him. He sees all things, all people, and all believers in all communities clearly. His vision is not blocked, cannot be blocked or dimmed by human ignorance or wisdom. He cannot compromise His standard and His judgment is without fear or favor.

On the Day of Judgment, you cannot stop Him. He will overthrow every opposition and tread under His feet all enemies of truth and righteousness.

> Then cometh the end, when he shall have delivered up the kingdom to God, even the Father; when he shall have put down all rule and all authority and power.
>
> For he must reign, till he hath put all enemies under his feet.
>
> The last enemy that shall be destroyed is death.
>
> For he hath put all things under his feet. But when he saith all things are put under him, it is manifest that he is excepted, which did put all things under him.

— 1 CORINTHIANS 15:24-27

Whatever you are doing in your community will end one day. Christ's letter is saying to you, do everything according to the rule. Your time will end one day. Your service will come to an end one day. You cannot occupy your position forever. You will be asked to give an account for your stewardship. The head of the community will call you for an account and nothing is hidden from His eyes.

You may be the boss, the master and an overseer. Jesus is saying; I am the Big Boss, the master of all masters and the highest overseer. He is going to ask you for an account and you cannot hide anything on that day. He sees all, knows all and can get to anywhere, and remind you even of those things you have forgotten.

He will put all rules, including your position to an end one day. Every power, including the one you are using now, will surrender to Christ. As a community leader, retired senior citizen, family head, prophet or prophetess, try to do everything according to the rule. Christ, the faithful Prophet, is the only one that His reign will last forever. Do not lead others as if you are the last overseer. If you choose to do things your own way, just know that one day Christ will put all enemies under His feet. Even death shall be destroyed on that day, how much less you and your witch doctors.

> For the Father judgeth no man, but hath committed all judgment unto the Son:
>
> — JOHN 5:22

> And he commanded us to preach unto the people, and to testify that it is he which was ordained of God to be the Judge of quick and dead.
>
> — ACTS 10:42

If there is anyone to be loyal to, it must be to Christ. Do not allow the fear of occult leaders from your community or church to put you at enmity with Christ. If you have to say no to anyone, let your no not be to Christ. Every judgment is committed to Christ by God, not to your earthly leaders.

Christ has the final say, not your charms. So, do everything to the glory of God and not to please people. If you die trying to do the right thing by obeying Christ, those who kill you cannot judge you anymore. The last judge you will meet after death is Christ, so do everything to please Him unto death.

Preach the way Christ asks you to preach, testify as He ordained you and do not misuse community funds to please your family. Do not compromise or remodel things wrongly to suit anyone except Christ. Fight the good fight, fulfill your ministry and please Christ to the end.

> In the day when God shall judge the secrets of men by Jesus Christ according to my gospel.
>
> — ROMANS 2:16

> But why dost thou judge thy brother? or why dost thou set at nought thy brother? for we shall all stand before the judgment seat of Christ.
>
> — ROMANS 14:10

Christ will not judge you according to your faithfulness to people but to His word. You must read His letters to the churches and do everything possible even unto death to obey His commands. He will not be bribed on the Day of Judgment and none can influence Him against you.

I charge thee therefore before God, and the Lord
Jesus Christ, who shall judge the quick and the dead
at his appearing and his kingdom;

— 2 TIMOTHY 4:1

If the community cult leader is fighting you because you are obeying God's word, Christ will reward you on the Day of Judgment. Every secret plot against you for obeying Christ will be exposed on the Day of Judgment. If you say the prayers now that are part of this program, the judgment can start now and you will be vindicated. No matter what it will cost you, don't ever disobey God's word, fight to the end.

TWO

PROGRESS IN YOUR COMMUNITY

A s I studied the seven letters to seven churches in Asia, I discovered to my shock and surprise that there is no place that you cannot achieve greatness. I also discovered that in every community you will find a mixture of good and evil, wheat and tares, the true and the false. The fact that some people made progress in the community of Thyatira is remarkable.

And unto the angel of the church in Thyatira write; These things saith the Son of God, who hath his eyes like unto a flame of fire, and his feet are like fine brass;

Saying, I am Alpha and Omega, the first and the last: and, what thou seest, write in a book, and send it unto the seven churches which are in Asia; unto Ephesus,

and unto Smyrna, and unto Pergamos, and unto
Thyatira, and unto Sardis, and unto Philadelphia, and
unto Laodicea.

— REVELATION 2:18; 1:11

Thyatira was an interesting little place located 30 miles from
Sadis and Pergamos. The city was built for one purpose – to act
as an interceptor to any army approaching Pergamos, the
capital of Asia Minor. It delayed any troops long enough to
allow Pergamos to get ready to fight them. It was a military
garrison to protect Pergamos. It also developed commercial
significance as it became the center of dyeing clothes, which
were sold in various parts of the known world.

And a certain woman named Lydia, a seller of purple,
of the city of Thyatira, which worshipped God, heard
us: whose heart the Lord opened, that she attended
unto the things which were spoken of Paul.

— ACTS 16:14

Lydia was fortunate to worship God in the city of Thyatira and
was prospered by God in purple business. The most important

assignment of every Christian is to discover their place in life and face what God has called them to do in righteousness.

People who complain of lack of progress must pray to discover their place in life, their relationship with God and their assignment on earth. Believers in Ephesus made progress in spite of the presence of the goddess, Diana. In Pergamos, a place described as the seat of Satan, the devil bowed to believers who lived in that city. They made progress and served God in truth and in spirit.

Serving lays the foundation for true progress. Many believers are not serving God, yet they complain of lack of progress. There is no community too good or too bad to stop any believer's progress if they remain steadfast in righteousness.

Many believers cannot challenge the seat of Satan where they are born. The believers in Thyatira were under the attack of a filthy prophetess but some committed members overcame the spirit of Jezebel in the woman and lived holy.

> I know thy works, and charity, and service, and faith, and thy patience, and thy works; and the last to be more than the first.
>
> — REVELATION 2:19

16

They were able to discern and know the right people to be helped. They were charitable, and served with faithfulness to the end. It was not easy for them at the initial stage but they were patient enough to wait for God's time. The problem with many believers is lack of patience. They are carnal and do not bear the fruits of the spirit.

> But the fruit of the Spirit is love, joy, peace, longsuffering, gentleness, goodness, faith,
>
> Meekness, temperance: against such there is no law.
>
> — GALATIANS 5:22-23

When you love God, His word and work, you can face any battle. The love of God will compel you to stay where God assigned you and face the enemy. The joy of the victory ahead of you will motivate you to keep fighting, praying and believing in God to the end. You will not abandon your assignment in the church because of the fear of a filthy prophetess or an agent of the devil.

Unless you failed to discover your place in that church or city. But if you discover and face your divine call and love for God, you will surely make progress. Progress brings joy and joy from God leads to peace, settlement and establishment in life.

YOUR ROLE IN YOUR COMMUNITY

To make progress anywhere you find yourself, you have to be steadfast, and committed to your divine assignment unto the end. To achieve this, you must be born again and manifest the fruits of long suffering which will lead you to greatness. With the above, you will make progress. You will live a gentle life and faithfully serve God with what He has blessed you with.

Once you settle where God has called you, meek spiritedness and temperance will be your definition. Many need to prayerfully cast out the spirit of vagabond and fugitive from their life.

You need to discover your place in life, know your divine assignment and fearlessly fight residential powers. You need to discover the filthy prophetess, the agents of defilement and destruction and fight them in other to make progress (Job 17:9; Psalm 84:9).

When you discover your place and divine assignment, the next battle is to establish a permanent relationship with God and His children. This will deliver you from evil associations and from agents of the devil. With that, you will discover and reject the evil influence of the filthy prophetess, filthy people and satanic agents.

The victorious believers in Thyatira kept to God's way, and refused to be influenced and polluted by the filthy prophetess in their midst. They made progress and God blessed the works of their hands.

Some had their progress delayed, stopped and attacked but they never compromised. They kept their relationship with God and kept serving God. It was not easy for them to worship God in a place where the filthy prophetess ruled but they persisted to the end.

One day, they gained strength. Victory was achieved and they made progress. They received deliverance, achieved greatness and lived for Christ in the city of Thyatira. The strength of the Thyatira came from God, the prophecy came from God and the deliverance came from God.

Today, the question everywhere is: Can your pastor prophesy, see vision, heal or deliver me? No one is interested in the source of the prophecy, the power or the anointing. Once someone can prophecy, you will see crowds and great multitudes following him.

THREE

DISCERNING FALSE PROPHETS

There are very few today who seek for God's word or righteous pastors with clean hands. In order to keep and get new members, and to prophesy, many pastors have defiled their hands.

Every pastor wants to be a prophet or prophetess. Very few are still holding on to the way of the Lord. Many have left the way of righteous living. They have polluted their hands and co-operated with the devil for fake power and prosperity.

They have left Christ, and forsaken the truth for filthy prophecies from the dark kingdom. Many pastors need deliverance from the spirit of Jezebel and her mother, the woman that sits upon many waters.

And I saw the woman drunken with the blood of the saints, and with the blood of the martyrs of Jesus: and when I saw her, I wondered with great admiration.

And he saith unto me, the waters which thou sawest, where the whore sitteth, are peoples, and multitudes, and nations, and tongues.

—   REVELATION 17:6, 15

THE WOMAN IN CHARGE OF FALSEHOOD

This is the woman that distributes fake powers and the spirit of Jezebel. Many ministers are guilty and they need deliverance with the members of their congregation. This woman, the mother of Jezebel, has made many walking corpses.

She has killed many ministers and drank their blood while they are alive. She gives ministers the power to sit upon their ministries, health, business, and finances and upon their members. Many ministers have sold their lives, ministries and even their members to this evil woman. That is why many people in the church are suffering, and dying in their problems without help.

> And he saith unto me, the waters which thou sawest, where the whore sitteth, are peoples, and multitudes, and nations, and tongues.
>
> — REVELATION 17:15

She is sitting upon destinies, marriages, health, and the greatness of many. Many great ministers, ministries and center their members need deliverance but they do not know how to go about it.

Their source of power is fake, filthy and demonic. Their members are in trouble and under the yoke of filthy prophets, prophetesses and ministers.

> And Jabez called on the God of Israel, saying, oh that thou wouldest bless me indeed, and enlarge my coast, and that thine hand might be with me, and that thou wouldest keep me from evil, that it may not grieve me! And God granted him that which he requested.
>
> — 1 CHRONICLES 4:10

> But the path of the just is as the shining light, that shineth more and more unto the perfect day.
>
> — PROVERBS 4:18

> Enlarge the place of thy tent, and let them stretch forth the curtains of thine habitations: spare not, lengthen thy cords, and strengthen thy stakes;
>
> — ISAIAH 54:2

The family of Jabez changed their pattern of family prayer through Jabez. You need to change the pattern of your prayers. You need to seek deliverance from ministers who still keep clean hands. You need to call upon Christ directly. He is the true and faithful Prophet with power to deliver you from every captivity.

This letter is an avenue to link you up with the true Prophet, the great deliverer and the coming king. This is time to leave darkness and come to the true light which is Christ. You can ask for personal deliverance now and get it. You have the opportunity to get your deliverance directly from Christ right away.

No matter how much you have backslidden or gone astray from the true light, you can come back. Christ is the true Prophet and you can receive prophecies directly from Him now. There is no place you are that Christ cannot reach and deliver you if only you ask for deliverance sincerely.

> And Samuel spake unto all the house of Israel, saying, if ye do return unto the Lord with all your hearts, then put away the strange gods and Ashtaroth from among you, and prepare your hearts unto the Lord, and serve him only: and he will deliver you out of the hand of the Philistines.

> Then the children of Israel did put away Baalim and Ashtaroth, and served the Lord only.
>
> — 1 SAMUEL 7:3-4

You can still make progress in every area of your life. Some of the prophets and prophetesses you run to are not real nor better than you. They are agents of the devil and under deceit to deceive others. Jesus is the only true and faithful Prophet.

Some of the prophetesses and prophets are in covenant with the devil and the woman that sits upon many waters. They can prophesy, and tell you stories but cannot cast out the spirit behind your problems. They can tell you half-truths but they lack the power to deliver you out of troubles.

Let me tell you what some of them do. They are in covenant with the devil to sanction or suspend your problems for some time. They do not cast out demons or solve problems. Others with the power of fake prophecy, like the woman in our text called Jezebel, can see but cannot proffer solutions. Others, in the third group, transfer demons or problems from legs to hands, head to business, father to mother or anywhere.

Some of these prophets, prophetesses and ministers you run after operate with the under-listed triple "S".

They:

1. Sanction or suspend problems for a season.

2. See problems and define them without bringing permanent solutions.

3. Send your problem from one area of your life to another.

They are worse than the prophetess in the book of Revelation. Our text called Jezebel a filthy prophetess. In the school of deliverance, we call them prophets, prophetesses and ministers with triple S. They are deceivers. They operate with the counterfeits from Satan.

> For such are false apostles, deceitful workers, transforming themselves into the apostles of Christ. And no marvel; for Satan himself is transformed into an angel of light. Therefore, it is no great thing if his ministers also be transformed as the ministers of righteousness; whose end shall be according to their works.
>
> — 2 CORINTHIANS 11:13-15

Some of them can prophesy but their lives are filled with greed, pride, anger, immorality, covetousness, financial irresponsibility, jealousy, unfaithfulness, occultism and all manner of fleshly lusts. They are swindlers, and carnal without any robe of righteousness.

FOUR

VICTORY OVER SATANIC PROPHETS

S ome believers in the church at Thyatira overcame the filthy prophetess and Christ commended them for their spiritual progress. They overcame her by bearing the fruits of the spirit. They had true love for Christ and served with patience and endurance to the end.

Though the church in Thyatira lacked sound doctrine by tolerating the false prophetess but some members overcame her evil teaching and way of life. Some prophets are sorcerers and magicians. Their rods of power are not from God but they can produce serpents or temporary miracles and testimonies.

They are swindlers. They act like lambs but speak like Dragons (2 Corinthians 11:13-15; John 14:12; Matthew 7:15).

They are commercial and carnal in nature; filled with the love of money, covetousness, immorality, greed, pride, anger, and jealousy. What they prophesy to you concerning your occult uncle, neighbor, the strongman in your community or your enemies may be true. But if their own occult source of power is low, your occult uncle's power may swallow their rods, and render the prayers they said for you ineffectual. At that point, you will lose your miracles, testimonies and other benefits of their enchantments.

The next thing is that you become subject to satanic attacks for challenging a higher occult power. Your situation may prove worse than before their so-called liberation or deliverance was carried out.

If the false prophet that prayed for you has higher occult powers than the powers against you, your problems may be suspended, transferred or sanctioned for a season. They never cast out demons because demons cannot cast out demons.

TRAINING SCHOOL FOR TRUE LIBERATION

Anyone determined to go through liberation with result must pass through the school of OBEDIENCE. They must go through some teachings before undergoing deliverance. They must humble themselves before a seasoned born-again teacher who will share the truth and nothing but the truth with them like I am telling you now.

BIBLE PASSAGES TO READ

The meaning of covenants and the need for faithfulness in covenants

(Genesis 21:32; 1 Samuel 11:1-2; Exodus 23:32; 34:12, 15; Hosea 12:1).

The types of covenants

(Genesis 12:1-3; 2 Kings 3:26-27).

How covenants are confirmed

(Hebrews 6:13-17; Psalm 105:8-10; Galatians 3:15).

Obedience and blessings in obedience

(Exodus 19:5-6; Deuteronomy 11:8-9; 28:1-14; Joshua 1:5-8; 1 Kings 3:14-15; 1 Chronicles 28:9-10; 2 Chronicles 15:1-2; Isaiah 1:16-20; 1 Samuel 15:22; 1 Peter 1:14-16; 4:17-19; Hebrews 5:8-9).

God's faithfulness in keeping covenants

(Genesis 12:7; 13:15; 17:7-8; Joshua 21:43-45).

The consequences of breaking covenants

(Deuteronomy 28:15-68; Joshua 9:15, 22-23, 27; 2 Samuel 21:1-9; Lamentation 5:1-7).

Calls to break covenants with the devil and enter into covenants with God through Christ

(Isaiah 45:22; 55:1-3; Ezekiel 33:11; Matthew 11:28-30; 23:37; John 1:29; 3:16-17; 4:42; Romans 5:18; 2 Corinthians 5:14-15, 18-19; 1 Timothy 2:4-6; 4:10; 2 Peter 3:9; Hebrews 2:9; 1 John 2:2; Revelation 22:17).

The doctrine of forgiveness

(Matthew 18:15-35; 20:24-28; Mark 11:25-26; Luke 6:35-37; 1 Corinthians 6:1; Ephesians 4:32; Colossians 3:13; Luke 17:3-5).

God's commandment to forgive

(Matthew 5:39-46; 6:12, 14, 15; Matthew 18:21-22; Romans 12:14, 17, 19, 21; Mark 11:25-26).

The life of obedience, authority and warfare

(2 Corinthians 10:3-6; Mark 16:15-18; Luke 10:18-20; 9:1; John 14:12-14; Matthew 18:18-19).

Spiritual weapons

(Zechariah 4:6; Isaiah 40:28-31; James 4:6-7; 1 Peter 5:8-9; 2 Corinthians 12:9; Hebrews 11:33-34; Ephesians 6:13-18).

Resisting temptations and promise of victory

(Matthew 26:41; Proverbs 1:10-15; Job 2:9-10; Jeremiah 35:5-6; Daniel 1:8; Romans 6:13; 2 Peter 3:17; Luke 4:5-8 and 1

Corinthians 10:13; Hebrews 2:18; 4:13-16; Philippians 4:8; Ephesians 6:10-18; 2 Peter 2:9).

The call, prayer, promise and provision for holiness

(1 Thessalonians 4:7, 8; Hebrews 2:11; 10:10; 13:12-13; Ephesians 5:25-27; John 17:17-21; 1 Thessalonians 5:23-24).

WARFARE SECTION

DECREES FOR DELIVERANCE FROM PERSONAL IDOL

Any root of idolatry in my life, be uprooted, in the name of Jesus. Blood of Jesus, flow into my foundation and deliver me from idolatry, in the name of Jesus.

Every enemy of my relationship with God, be destroyed, in the name of Jesus. O Lord, arise and deliver me from the power of idolatry, in the name of Jesus.

I loose myself from the power of religion without Christ, in the name of Jesus. Any false god controlling my life, release me by force, in the name of Jesus. Every god I made for myself, I reject you, in the name of Jesus.

Every god I inherited from anywhere, I reject you by force, in the name of Jesus. Any deity assigned to waste my life, catch fire, in the name of Jesus. Any power blocking me from the true God, disappear, in the name of Jesus.

Father Lord, help me to worship you with all my heart, in the name of Jesus. Any idol of possession, plenty, and pride in my life, be frustrated, in the name of Jesus. I command the powers of the idol of pleasure and money in my life to die, in the name of Jesus.

Every problem that idolatry has brought into my life, die by force, in the name of Jesus. Any satanic programme in my life because of idolatry, be terminated, in the name of Jesus.

DECREES AGAINST FAMILY IDOLS

Any god in my family standing as the true God, I expose and reject you, in the name of Jesus. Any god promoting abomination in my family, I reject you, in the name of Jesus.

I break and loose myself from covenants of my family idol, in the name of Jesus. Father Lord, empower me to hate my family idol with great hatred, in the name of Jesus. I break and loose myself from family vanities, in the name of Jesus. I break and loose myself from every unprofitable relationship, in the name of Jesus.

Any covenant linking me to my family idol, break, in the name of Jesus. Any curse in my life from my family idol, expire, in the name of Jesus. Blood of Jesus, speak me out of my family idol, in the name of Jesus. Any problem in my life from my family idol, expire, in the name of Jesus.

Every yoke of bondage from my family idol, break, in the name of Jesus. Holy Ghost fire, burn between me and my family idol, in the name of Jesus. Any foolishness in my life from my family idol, die, in the name of Jesus.

Any bad thing I inherited from my family idol, I reject you now, in the name of Jesus. Father Lord, deliver me completely from my family idols, in the name of Jesus.

DECREES AGAINST COMMUNITY IDOLS

I break and loose myself from the arrest of my community idols, in the name of Jesus. Any satanic net fashioned against me from my community idol, catch fire, in the name of Jesus.

O Lord, walk me out of my community idol, in the name of Jesus. Every demon attached to my community idols, I am no longer your candidate, in the name of Jesus.

O Lord, give me the enablement to live above my community idols, in the name of Jesus. Every weapon of my community idol against me, be rendered impotent, in the name of Jesus.

Every property of my community idol in my life, catch fire, in the name of Jesus. Any evil hand upon my life from my community idol, wither, in the name of Jesus.

Set me free O Lord, from the power of my community idol, in the name of Jesus. O Lord, by the power in the blood of Jesus, remove me from the problems from my community idols, in the name of Jesus. I break to pieces the backbone of my community strongman, in the name of Jesus.

Any evil monitor from my community, be blinded, in the name of Jesus. Any evil invitation from my community idol, I reject you, in the name of Jesus. Every evil handover of my life to the community idol, I reject you, in the name of Jesus. Every attack against me from my community idol, stop by force, in the name of Jesus.

DECREES AGAINST COLLECTIVE CAPTIVITY

I break and loose myself from every collective captivity, in the name of Jesus. Every collective problem assigned to waste my life, be wasted, in the name of Jesus.

O hand of God, take me away from all manner of captivities, in the name of Jesus. Any personal invitation given to any power against me, I withdraw you by force, in the name of Jesus. Any evil power on assignment over my life, be blinded, in the name of Jesus.

Ancient of days, deliver me from every collective captivity, in the name of Jesus. Any power from any altar that has arrested me, release me now, in the name of Jesus. Every inherited bondage in my life, break into pieces, in the name of Jesus.

Every arrow of common death fired against my life, backfire, in the name of Jesus. O Lord, arise and take me away from demonic captivity, in the name of Jesus. Any satanic prison locking me up, open and release me, in the name of Jesus.

Any plan of the enemy involving me for mass destruction, fail, in the name of Jesus. Holy Ghost fire, burn to ashes every property of collective captivity in my life, in the name of Jesus.

I disarm evil powers assigned to waste my destiny, in the name of Jesus. Angels of the Living God, walk me out of any collective bondage, in the name of Jesus. Every danger ahead of me, disappear before my arrival, in the name of Jesus.

DECREES AGAINST TRIBAL IDOLS

Every covenant with tribal idols in my life, break by force, in the name of Jesus. Every curse of tribal idol in my life, expire, in the name of Jesus. Every idol of my place of birth, release me by force, in the name of Jesus.

I break and loose myself from the embargoes of my tribal idols, in the name of Jesus. Power to walk away for freedom from my tribal idols; possess me, in the name of Jesus. Any limitation in my life from my family idol, disappear, in the name of Jesus.

Any tribal sin in my life, I reject you by force, in the name of Jesus. Any evil and problems from my tribal idols, die, in the name of Jesus. I break and loose myself from my tribal bondage, in the name of Jesus. Every evil chain holding me down in my tribe, break, in the name of Jesus.

Blood of Jesus, speak me out of every tribal limitation, in the name of Jesus. O Lord, promote me above my tribal full stops, in the name of Jesus. Every tribal disgrace, shame, and reproach in my life, die, in the name of Jesus.

All satanic program for my tribe, I reject you now, in the name of Jesus. Every evil device against me by my tribal demons, fail woefully, in the name of Jesus.

DECREES AGAINST ALL PROBLEMS

Every idol that has taken me into captivity, release me by force, in the name of Jesus. Any problem in my life from any idol, die by fire, in the name of Jesus. Every demonic full stop in my life from satanic altars, disappear, in the name of Jesus. Any evil covenant in my life from any altar, break, in the name of Jesus.

Every curse in my life from any evil altar, expire, in the name of Jesus. Every sinful character in my life from any evil altar, be uprooted, in the name of Jesus. O Lord, arise and deliver me from every problem from any idol, in the name of Jesus. Healing power of God, overshadow me inside and outside, in the name of Jesus.

Any vessel sent against me from any evil altar, be wasted, in the name of Jesus. Any evil tongue attacking me from any evil altar, I cut you off, in the name of Jesus. Any personal invitation given to me from evil altar, I reject you, in the name of Jesus.

Every wicked action taken against me from any evil altar, fail, in the name of Jesus. Any problem that has converted my right hand to left hand, die, in the name of Jesus. Any evil kingdom assigned against me, scatter, in the name of Jesus. Let the strongman fall into the pit they dug for me, in the name of Jesus.

All my blessings swallowed by evil people, be vomited now, in the name of Jesus. Father Lord, command every problem in my life to disappear, in the name of Jesus.

DECREES TO OVERTHROW MEDIOCRITY

Father Lord, arise and overthrow mediocrity in this city, in the name of Jesus. Every enemy of meritocracy in this town, be frustrated, in the name of Jesus. You spirit of Herod in this place, be disgraced, in the name of Jesus. Every Goliath boasting in this land, receive confusion, in the name of Jesus.

Every evil covenant to dethrone God's children in this place, break, in the name of Jesus. Every limitation placed upon God's people in this place; disappear, in the name of Jesus. Let the sacrifice of the occult in this place backfire, in the name of Jesus. Every evil imagination against God's children, backfire, in the name of Jesus.

Every curse placed upon God's children in this land, backfire, in the name of Jesus. Blood of Jesus, speak your children out of every bondage, in the name of Jesus. Heavenly Father, overthrow all the wickedness in this land, in the name of Jesus.

Let those laughing at God's children in this town be disgraced, in the name of Jesus. Every destructive plan of the enemy in this community, blow up in their faces, in the name of Jesus. I command the point of ridicule against believers to be converted to promotion, in the name of Jesus. Every Pharaoh in this community, be destroyed by Red Sea, in the name of Jesus.

DECREES TO PROSPER IN ANY COMMUNITY

I break and loose myself from every foundational bondage, in the name of Jesus. Every yoke of poverty in my life, break to pieces, in the name of Jesus. O Lord, arise and bless the works of my hands, in the name of Jesus. Every enemy of my prosperity, be frustrated, in the name of Jesus.

Every yoke of backwardness in my life, break, in the name of Jesus. Any strongman against my prosperity in this land, be paralyzed, in the name of Jesus. Every messenger of failure against my work, be frustrated, in the name of Jesus. Every organized darkness against my efforts, be disorganized, in the name of Jesus.

Every agent of shame in my life, in this place, be disappointed, in the name of Jesus. Let the activity of the enemy against me backfire, in the name of Jesus. Any strange fire, burning against my prosperity, be quenched, in the name of Jesus.

O Lord, empower me for maximum achievement in this land, in the name of Jesus. Let the powers of the enemy against me in this town fail, in the name of Jesus. Anointing to prosper in this town, possess me now, in the name of Jesus.

Every chain of unfruitfulness placed upon me, be broken, in the name of Jesus. Every arrow of death fired against me, backfire, in the name of Jesus.

DECREES AGAINST OCCULTISM

Every evil gathering in this town, scatter in shame, in the name of Jesus. Let all the occult groups in this community be disorganized, in the name of Jesus. Any evil sacrifice going on in this land, be rejected, in the name of Jesus.

Let the head of the occult in this town be cut off, in the name of Jesus. Blood of Jesus, speak death unto the occults in this town, in the name of Jesus. Every occult agreement in this community, fail woefully, in the name of Jesus. Heavenly Father, arise and destroy occultism in this town, in the name of Jesus.

Fire of God, burn to ashes every weapon of occultism in this town, in the name of Jesus. Every evil spirit behind occultism in this town, be cast out, in the name of Jesus. Every curse placed upon the city by occultist, backfire, in the name of Jesus.

Every door opened by occultism in this land, be closed, in the name of Jesus. Every messenger of the devil in this city, be disgraced, in the name of Jesus. Let the brains of the occults in this land scatter in confusion, in the name of Jesus. Every messenger of death raised by the occults in this land, kill your owners, in the name of Jesus.

DECREES AGAINST UNREPENTANT KILLERS

Every weapon of the murderers in this land, kill your owners, in the name of Jesus. Every unrepentant agent in this land, die by your own weapons, in the name of Jesus. Every murderer in this town, repent or perish, in the name of Jesus. Holy Ghost fire, burn to ashes, every weapon of death, in the name of Jesus.

Every arrow of death fired against my life, backfire, in the name of Jesus. I deliver and pass-out every satanic food from unrepentant murderers, in the name of Jesus. Let all the evil manipulations from all the unrepentant murderer fail, in the name of Jesus. I withdraw my life from unrepentant murderers, in the name of Jesus.

Architecture of the enemy against me to kill me, die in my place, in the name of Jesus. Any plan to kill me in the dream, fail woefully, in the name of Jesus. Every poison prepared to waste my life, waste your owner, in the name of Jesus.

Any satanic agent trying to kill people's destiny in this land, kill yourself, in the name of Jesus. Let all destiny killers in this land be frustrated, in the name of Jesus. Every destructive weapon destroying in this town, destroy your owner, in the name of

Jesus. O Lord, turn the weapons of death against every unrepentant enemy, in the name of Jesus.

DECREES AGAINST STRONGMAN

You the strongman in this land, repent or perish, in the name of Jesus. Every messenger of the devil in this land, swallow confusion, in the name of Jesus. Let the strongman in charge of sin and problems in this land be wasted, in the name of Jesus.

O Lord, chain every strongman in this community with your chains, in the name of Jesus. Any soul in this land captured by any strongman, be released, in the name of Jesus. Every blessing in this land captured by evil men, be released, in the name of Jesus.

Angels of the Living God, enter into the strongman's house and release all his captives, in the name of Jesus. Divine judgment, fall upon the head of the strongman, in the name of Jesus. Every charm of the strongman in the city, lose your power, in the name of Jesus.

Every sacrifice of the strongman, expire, in the name of Jesus. Lord Jesus, deliver everyone from the bondage of the strongman, in the name of Jesus. Let all the agent of the strongman rise against him, in the name of Jesus. Arrows of the strongman, backfire, in the name of Jesus.

I command the strongman to work against himself from now, in the name of Jesus. Let every strongman submit his or her power and surrender to Jesus, in the name of Jesus. Every determined unrepentant strongman, die with your weapons, in the name of Jesus.

DECREES FOR DIVINE PRESENCE

O Lord, appear in this community and take over, in the name of Jesus. Let every evil in this land be terminated, in the name of Jesus. Every demonic weakness in this community, be converted to divine strength, in the name of Jesus.

Let all evil leaders in this town be exposed and disgraced, in the name of Jesus. Father Lord, overthrow all evil leaders in this land, in the name of Jesus. Every enemy of God in this land, turn against yourselves, in the name of Jesus.

I command every captive in this community to be released, in the name of Jesus. Every wickedness going on in this land, be terminated, in the name of Jesus. I command every witchcraft in this land to backfire, in the name of Jesus. O Lord, raise great men in this town to rule the nation, in the name of Jesus.

Holy Ghost fire, burn to ashes every evil investment in this land, in the name of Jesus. Let divine doors begin to open in this land, in the name of Jesus. Every enemy of progress in this community, be exposed and disgraced, in the name of Jesus.

Enemies of God's children in this land, receive your rewards by force, in the name of Jesus. Every destiny killer in this town, be wasted, in the name of Jesus.

DECREES FOR YOUR DELIVERANCE

O Lord, deliver me from occultism of my place of birth, in the name of Jesus. Powers of sin, lose your hold over my life forever, in the name of Jesus. Every chain of poverty in my life, break to pieces in the name of Jesus.

Every demon attacking me from any altar, I bind you forever, in the name of Jesus. I walk out from every collective captivity, in the name of Jesus. Every idol controlling my life, lose your power, in the name of Jesus. I command every satanic limitation in my life to disappear, in the name of Jesus.

Any evil covenant keeping me in bondage, break, in the name of Jesus. All problems in my life, the door is open; rush out forever, in the name of Jesus. O Lord, prosper me in this land, in the name of Jesus. I command prosperity to magnetize my life everywhere I go, in the name of Jesus.

Let every charm of the wicked fail in my life, in the name of Jesus. O Lord, help me to be conscious of your presence at all time, in the name of Jesus. Every danger waiting for me anywhere, vanish before my arrival, in the name of Jesus. O Lord, arise and fight my battles everywhere, in the name of Jesus. Father Lord, appear before my Goliaths, in the name of Jesus.

DECREES FOR PEACE IN THE LAND

Every agent of confusion in this land, receive double frustration, in the name of Jesus. I command the divine programme for this community to appear, in the name of Jesus. Let all the troublemakers in this land be troubled by troubles, in the name of Jesus.

No child of God will live below their standard, in the name of Jesus. Any evil personality promoting problems in this community, repent or die, in the name of Jesus. Every demonic activity going on in this land, stop by force, in the name of Jesus.

Every messenger of death in this community, carry your message to your sender, in the name of Jesus. Prince of peace, bring perfect peace in this community, in the name of Jesus. Every enemy of peace in this land, repent or die in pieces, in the name of Jesus.

Any satanic movement in this community, be demobilized, in the name of Jesus. Every satanic re-arrangement in this land, I reject you, in the name of Jesus. Any evil personalities re-drawing the map of people in this land, repent or die, in the name of Jesus. Every destiny polluter in this land, be polluted unto destruction, in the name of Jesus.

Every damage done against this community, receive repair, in the name of Jesus. Any strongman converting people to rags in this land, repent or die, in the name of Jesus. Peace like river, flow into this community from now, in the name of Jesus.

Every enemy of this community, be exposed and disgraced, in the name of Jesus. Let the foundation of this community quake for peace, in the name of Jesus. Every mountain standing against peace in this land, be removed by force, in the name of Jesus.

Any evil personality converting evil for good and good for evil, repent or perish, in the name of Jesus. Any evil hand upon this land, wither by fire, in the name of Jesus. Let all powers of darkness assigned to trouble this land be troubled, in the name of Jesus.

Every tree of trouble planted in this land, be uprooted, in the name of Jesus. I convert every trouble in this land into peace, in the name of Jesus. Every weapon of trouble in this land, catch fire, in the name of Jesus. Let death kill every trouble in this community today, in the name of Jesus.

Lord Jesus, take over this land, in the name of Jesus. Holy Ghost fire, burn all over this land, in the name of Jesus. Blood of Jesus, speak peace unto this land, in the name of Jesus. Father Lord, bring everlasting peace into this community, in the name of Jesus.

DECREES OF JUDGMENT IN THE LAND

Powers behind multiple evil covenants in this community, die, in the name of Jesus. Powers behind iron-like curses and stubborn problems, be cast out, in the name of Jesus. Every dark angel released into this town, disappear, in the name of Jesus.

Messengers of rain of affliction in this town, repent or die in affliction, in the name of Jesus. Any powers expanding the problems in this town, be wasted, in the name of Jesus. Let the spirit of death and hell fire be cast out of this town, in the name of Jesus.

Any power contending with my angel of blessing, fall down and die, in the name of Jesus. Any evil eye observing this town, be blinded, in the name of Jesus. Spirit of love of money in this town, I cast you out, in the name of Jesus. Every yoke of backward progress diverting prosperity in this town, break, in the name of Jesus.

Let all progress diverters in this community be exposed and disgraced, in the name of Jesus. Evil mark placed upon this community, be removed, in the name of Jesus. Let all witchcraft handwriting be roasted by fire, in the name of Jesus. I command all-star hijackers in this community to repent or die, in the name of Jesus.

Spirit of vagabond upon the people of this community, I cast you out, in the name of Jesus. Every evil spy in this town, be blinded by fire, in the name of Jesus. Every unrepentant head manipulator in this town, repent or run mad, in the name of Jesus.

Any power that has arrested the progress of this town, release it by force, in the name of Jesus. O Lord, arise and deliver the people of this community from coffin spirit, in the name of Jesus. You my arrested greatness and destiny, be released, in the name of Jesus.

Divine unbearable heat; destroy every unrepentant enemy in this land, in the name of Jesus. Let demonic merciless worms eat up every unrepentant agent against the land, in the name of Jesus. Let every wicked person in this land repent or face double destruction, in the name of Jesus.

Whirlwind of disappointments, confusion and destructive oppressions, waste the wasters in this land, in the name of Jesus. Anger of God, fall upon every unrepentant wicked in this land, in the name of Jesus. Any occult grandmaster thinking evil against the community, receive brain disorder, in the name of Jesus.

Any evil personality polluting people's life in this community in the dreams, be roasted by fire of God, in the name of Jesus.

Let anyone feeding people in the dreams with poisoned foods, eat your foods and drink your drinks, in the name of Jesus.

Any covenant against God's children in this community, break and backfire, in the name of Jesus. Whoever has vowed to kill me in this community, kill yourself alone, in the name of Jesus. Any good thing in my life arrested in any evil altar, be release by force, in the name of Jesus.

THANK YOU!

I'd like to use this time to thank you for purchasing my books and helping my ministry and work. Any copy of my book you buy helps to fund my ministry and family, as well as offering much-needed inspiration to keep writing. My family and I are very thankful, and we take your assistance very seriously.

You have already accomplished so much, but I would appreciate an honest review of some of my books through the link below. This is critical since reviews reflect how much an author's work is respected.

Please visit https://www.amazon.com/review/create-review?asin=B0B4K6Y63B or CLICK HERE TO LEAVE A REVIEW

Please be aware that I read and value all comments and reviews. You can always post a review even though you haven't finished the book yet, and then edit your reviews later.

Once again, here is the link:

Please visit https://www.amazon.com/review/create-review?asin=B0B4K6Y63B or CLICK HERE TO LEAVE A REVIEW

Thank you so much as you spare a precious moment of your time and may God bless you and meet you at the very point of your need.

You can also send me an email to prayermadu@yahoo.com if you encounter any difficulty while writing your review.

PRAYER MADUEKE'S
TOP 50 BESTSELLING BOOKS

(Click on any of them to view them on Amazon)

1. Speaking Things Into Existence by Faith

2. Praying With the Blood of Jesus

3. The Hidden Supernatural Power in Fasting and Prayer

4. Monitoring Spirits

5. Dictionary of Demons & Complete Deliverance

6. Reversing Satanic Judgments in Heavenly Courts

7. The Reality of Spirit Marriage

8. Defeating the Python Spirit

9. Discerning and Defeating the Ahab & Jezebel Spirit

10. Evil Presence

11. Queen of Heaven

12. Leviathan the Beast

13. Command the Morning, Day and Night

14. Evil Summon

15. 35 Special Dangerous Decrees

16. Releasing Destinies From the Courts of Heaven

17. The Battle Plan For Destroying Foundational Witchcraft

18. Total Destruction and Dominion Over Water Spirits

19. Breaking Evil Yokes

20. Power to Pray Once and Receive Answers

21. When Evil Altars Are Multiplied

22. Prayers to Receive Financial Miracles

23. 21/40 Nights of Decrees and Your Enemies Will Surrender

24. Destroying Evil Marks

25. 91 Days Decrees to Takeover the Year

26. Organized Darkness

27. The Battle Plan For Destroying Foundational Occultism

28. Divine Protection & Immunity While Sleeping

29. Dominion Over Sickness & Disease

30. Dangerous Decrees to Destroy Your Destroyers

31. 100 Days Prayers to Wake Up Your Lazarus

32. Idolatry

33. Prayers Against Satanic Oppression

34. Prayers for Financial Breakthrough

35. Prayers to Marry Without Delay

36. Prayers for Protection

37. The Power of Speaking in Tongues

38. Healing Covenant

39. Dictionary of Unmerited Favor

40. Prayers to Marry Without Delay

41. The Operation of the Woman That Sits Upon Many Waters

42. Your Dream Directory

43. Dangerous Decrees to Destroy Your Destroyers

44. Prayers for Breakthrough in Your Business

45. The Queen of the Coast

46. The Philosophy of Deliverance

47. Prayers for Mercy

48. Prayers for Children and Youths

49. Comprehensive Deliverance

50. A Jump From Evil Altar

FREE EBOOKS

In order to say a 'Thank You' for purchasing *The False Prophet*, I offer these books to you in appreciation.

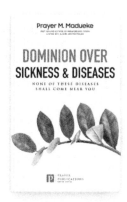
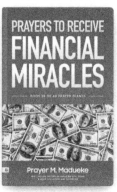

> **Click here or go to madueke.com/free-gift to download the eBooks now** <

CHRISTIAN COUNSELLING

We were created for a greater purpose than only survival and God wants us to live a full life.

If you need prayer or counselling, or if you have any other inquiries, please visit the counselling page on my website madueke.com/counselling to know when I will be available for a phone call.

AN INVITATION TO BECOME A MINISTRY PARTNER

In response to several calls from readers of my books on how to collaborate with this ministry, we are grateful to provide our ministry's bank details.

Be assured that our continued prayers for you will be answered according to God's Word, and as you remain faithful by sowing seeds of faith, God will never forget your labors of love in Christ Jesus.

Send your Seeds to:

In Nigeria & Africa

Bank Name: **Access Bank**

Account Name: **Prayer Emancipation Missions**

Account Number: **0692638220**

In the United States & the rest of the World

Bank Name: **Bank of America**

Account Name: **Roseline C. Madueke**

Account Number: **483079070578**

You can also visit the donation page on my website to donate online: www.madueke.com/donate.

Printed in Great Britain
by Amazon

26684634R00046